Chalk or Cheese

The Calcium Cookbook

Gillian Greenwood

Copyright © 2023 by Gillian Greenwood, Audrey Goldberg, and Daria Archilei

This book and recipes are the intellectual property of Gillian Greenwood, Audrey Goldberg, Daria Archilei and may not be used, copied or reproduced in any form, without their prior consent

Disclaimer
To be safe, always check with your doctor before embarking on a diet change. The amounts of calcium found in the various recipes may vary.

CHALK or CHEESE?
www.ChalkOrCheese.com

Target Audience

Love browsing through cookery books and looking at dishes that are healthy and high in calcium?
Want to increase your calcium intake to improve your bones?
Been advised to take calcium supplements? Would you like an alternative?
Do you have osteopenia or osteoporosis?
Menopausal women - do you know which foods would benefit you?
Men are you over 50?

Then this book is for You!

Packed with delicious recipes to inspire you: Tart Wild Mushroom, Berry & Chia Seed Porridge, Vegan Curry to name just a few.

Why buy this book?

To avoid taking supplements (which can have health risks associated with them and it's always better to have the minerals naturally in food).

My book will take the headache out of working out which foods to eat to ensure 1,200mg of calcium in the diet.

Of course, if there is a medical reason for you to take calcium supplements you should always take your doctor's advice.

Foreword by Nick Panay

I am delighted to provide a foreword for this excellent book. As a menopause specialist, I regularly advise women to modify their diets to ensure that they include adequate calcium in order to provide protection against osteoporosis. However, it can be difficult for women to know what foods are the best and healthiest for them to obtain natural sources of calcium. Gillian Greenwood has taken this on board and through her experience and research has put together what I think is a very useful guide as to what the best natural sources of calcium are and has also included a number of exciting recipes to facilitate a calcium rich diet. Clearly this is not a replacement for medical advice where calcium levels are dangerously low, but I think this is an excellent opportunity for women to obtain sensible advice on this subject and to seek further advice where they remain at risk of low calcium which could potentially impact on their general wellbeing and in particular their bone strength. It is of course important that the correct balance is achieved as overdose of calcium can lead to significant side effects and risks and vitamins D and vitamin K also need to be considered to facilitate the absorption of calcium. All of this and more is covered in this excellent book, and I commend it to you.

Nick Panay BSc MBBS FRCOG MFSRH

Nick Panay is a Consultant Gynaecologist with a special interest in Reproductive Medicine, Menopause and Menstrual Disorders.

He works in the NHS and the private sector, holds an honorary academic appointment and is a Professor of Practice at Imperial College London and is the founder and director of Hormone Health, a company dedicated to women's healthcare.

Foreword by Nigel Denby

Women are in need of clear, practical advice when it comes to their bone health. Fear around menopause treatments, a fashion for dairy free diets and low levels of physical activity mean we are sitting on a bone health time bomb. Gillian Greenwood had written a well- researched, practical how to guide for eating well and living well for good bone health in midlife and the decades beyond. Bravo!

Nigel Denby BSc RD is an award-winning Registered Dietitian, with special clinical interests in Menopause, weight management and digestive health. He is author of ten successful nutrition books and a broadcaster across television and radio, both in the UK and Europe.

He is registered with the Health Professions Council and acts as Nutrition advisor to Women's Health Concern – the patient arm of the British Menopause Society.

About Gillian Greenwood and Why She Wrote This Book

Gillian Greenwood

I am a Pilates, yoga and ballet teacher. I have been teaching in Chelsea and surrounding areas in London UK for some 30 years and more recently on Zoom. This is my second book. In 2006 I wrote 'Pilates & Lifestyle with a Foreword by Julian Clary'.

I have always tried to eat healthily but first became interested in calcium after fracturing my foot in 2014. I was advised to take calcium supplements but decided to do some research on the internet. After a considerable time searching, I devised a way to eat the required daily 1,200mg* calcium instead of taking calcium supplements. (*mg is the abbreviation for milligrams.) I searched on the internet for books, calcium recipes and diets but couldn't find any. I then looked up which foods were high in calcium. It was a mammoth task. It is not easy to find foods that one can put into a daily diet. The values are sometimes quoted in 60mg, 100mg, a handful, sometimes as a cupful etc…! All were different values; impossible to compare without first calculating how much calcium in the same number of grams for all the foods. Something I thought might take a few minutes ended up taking days! To save you time and inconvenience I decided to write this book with Cordon Bleu Chef Audrey Goldberg and nutrition advisor Daria Archilei.

Table of Contents

Introduction	9
Types of Calcium Supplement	9
Increasing your Calcium Intake Made Simple	10
Reasons Why You Might Want to Increase Your Calcium Intake	11
Well-Balanced Diet	11
Vitamins, Minerals and Exercise	12
Exercise	14
How Much calcium Do We Need?	15
Calcium Fortified Foods v Calcium-rich Foods	16
Calcium Fortified Foods	16
Calcium-rich foods	16
Examples of Ways to Include 1,200mg of Calcium Daily	18
Recipes High in Calcium	23
Gillian's Recipes (The very quick ones)	**23**
All-Bran Breakfast	24
Muesli Breakfast	25
Salmon Avocado Salad	26
Cottage Cheese Green Beans Salad	27
Spicy Salmon Avocado	28
Strawberry Mousse	29
Daria Archilei's Recipes	**31**
Sardine Pasta	31
Vegan Curry	32
Fennel Salad	33
Caprese with Pesto	34
Prawns with Parsley Sauce Starter	35
Bruschetta with Goats Cheese & Tomatoes	36
Berry & Chia Seed Porridge	37
Ricotta Mousse with Almond Butter	39
Audrey Goldberg's Recipes	**40**
Pretty in Pink Prawns with Marie Rose Sauce	40
Scrambled Egg with Gravlax and Mascarpone	43

Tart Wild Mushroom	45
Salmon Theoule sur Mer with Gremolata	47
Affogato	49
Eastern Mess	51
Deconstructed Cheesecake with Figs	53
Salmon Rissoles	55
Tomato and Beans Salsa	57
Spaghetti Bolognese with Pesto	59
Pesto	61
Sardine Sarnie	62
Breakfast Bomb	63
Shakshuka	65
About the Authors	**68**
Gillian Greenwood	68
Audrey Goldberg	69
Daria Archilei	70
Recipes Index	**72**

Introduction

Which would you prefer to eat Chalk or Cheese? Ridiculous question you'd think, however every day many people are choosing to take calcium supplements which are in fact chalk! For many of these people there is an alternative to eating chalk and that is to eat cheese (also other calcium-rich food).

You may think well it's much easier to pop a few pills every day however, it's not certain how effective supplements are. They may have side effects, even health risks and not to mention the cost and remembering to take them twice a day every day for the rest of your life! This handy little guide will save you lots of time researching on the internet to see what your options are.

I know what you're thinking – Why is this book so short, it can't have much in it! Well, it will save you a lot of time – that's why this book is worth its weight in gold!

Types of Calcium Supplement

If you need to take a calcium supplement there are many types available: pills, capsules, liquids… to swallow, chew or drink… it can even be taken intravenously.

The most common calcium supplement is calcium carbonate, but there are other forms and if you suffer from constipation, you may decide that one of the other forms suits you better:

    Calcium carbonate
    Calcium citrate
    Calcium phosphate
    Calcium gluconate
    Calcium lactate
    Calcium chloride
    Coral calcium (calcium carbonate)

Increasing your Calcium Intake Made Simple

This is a short guide to help you increase your calcium intake. Your doctor might have carried out blood tests, noted that your calcium levels are below adequate and recommended that you take measures to improve this. Your doctor will tell you how many mg is appropriate for you.

There are 3 options:

1. Choose to swop some of your daily foods with others that are higher in calcium (this is the main aim of this guide).
2. Choose to add to your diet extra foods that are high in calcium (this will probably result in weight gain, which also comes with health risks).
3. Choose to take a calcium supplement daily (this could have health risks associated and may not be effective). Some people notice side effects, including constipation and kidney stones. Calcium supplements have also been linked to an increased chance of having a heart attack. You are unlikely to get these side effects from eating a normal amount of calcium as part of a healthy diet.

Consuming too much calcium in supplement form is dangerous to your health, however it would be very difficult to eat a balanced diet and consume too much calcium.

Reasons Why You Might Want to Increase Your Calcium Intake

There are many reasons why you might want to increase your calcium intake, the most common being that you are over 50 and have reduced bone mass resulting in weakened bones: Osteoporosis or less severe Osteopenia. After menopause, women will lose bone mass because they produce less oestrogen.

Perhaps you have suffered a low impact fracture (breaking a bone doing a very easy movement e.g. slipping off the kerb (as opposed to a high impact fracture e.g. falling badly whilst doing a bungee jump!).

You may have had a poor diet or taken medication with side effects that have resulted in impaired calcium levels; including long-term steroid medication and chemotherapy.

Other reasons for needing to increase your calcium are being **bed-bound, physical disability, Crohn's disease and Coeliac disease.**

Less Common - you may have suffered from **hyperparathyroidism.**

Well-Balanced Diet

It is important to include a variety of foods in your diet including vegetables, pasta, cereals, milk, dairy products, proteins: fish, meat, eggs, nuts, seeds and pulses.

Vitamins, Minerals and Exercise

In addition to increasing your calcium intake it is also important to consider including various vitamins and minerals in your diet as well as being active. Exercise will help your bones get stronger; this includes weight-bearing exercise e.g. walking.

Vitamin D

Vitamin D is fundamental element for calcium absorption. It is important to go outside during the daytime each day whether the sun is shining or not to absorb Vitamin D from the sunlight.

If the levels of Vitamin D in your blood are below the recommended level, your doctor may give you a prescription for Vitamin D. The doctor might prescribe calcium supplements combined with Vitamin D. You can talk to your doctor and mention increasing your calcium intake by changing your diet; in which case you will need to either get a prescription for Vitamin D on its own or buy them over the counter. Ask your doctor how many milligrams (mg) or units are appropriate for you to take daily. Vitamin D is available as a tablet, drops or mouth spray. There is a minty flavoured mouth spray available from health stores which I find particularly pleasant. The blue one 25mg (1000 units), is what I use - two sprays under my tongue; or the green one 75mg (3000 units) is one spray daily.

Boron

Boron is a trace mineral. That means that we only need a small amount of it. It helps our bodies to use calcium effectively. It is naturally present in most of the foods that we eat daily: oranges, mushrooms, almonds, pears, prunes, dates, grapes, cauliflower, broccoli, carrots, celery, raisins, dried apricots, avocados, apples, coffee, dried beans, peas, legumes, milk and potatoes.

Vitamin K

Vitamin K is a fat-soluble vitamin that the body requires in order to produce a protein called prothrombin, which promotes blood clotting and regulates bone metabolism.

The vitamin comes in two main forms:
1. Vitamin K-1, or phylloquinone, is present in dark leafy green vegetables and is the main dietary source of vitamin K.
2. Vitamin K-2, or menaquinone, is present in meats and fermented foods like:
   - natto (Japanese dish of fermented soya beans)
   - sauerkraut
   - dairy products, in particular hard cheeses
   - liver and organ meats
   - beef
   - pork
   - egg yolks
   - chicken

Gut bacteria also produce vitamin K-2.

Vitamin K-2 supports healthy bone mineral density with carboxylating osteocalcin, a protein that is a key regulator of calcium usage. Vitamin K2 supplement may be beneficial for preventing osteoporosis.

Exercise

Using your muscles for weight-bearing exercise helps you protect your bones. Many activities are weight bearing, swimming would not be included because the water takes your weight. See below for ways you can do this without joining a gym.
- Strength training (using body weight e.g. press ups and hand weights e.g. bicep curls).
- Weight bearing aerobic exercise e.g. walking, jogging, running.
- Weight bearing anaerobic exercise e.g. playing tennis.
- Flexibility exercises e.g. touching your toes, should be included to keep your muscles lengthened.
- Stability and balance exercises e.g. standing on one leg, should be included to reduce the risk of falls leading to fractures.

Personally, I like to walk as much as possible because it is such a good weight-bearing exercise. Sometimes I get off the bus/tube early so that I can walk the rest of the way. Most phones have a step counter included and it is very encouraging to make a note of how many steps you take each day. 7,000 steps a day is considered to be healthy and 10,000 would be particularly beneficial.

How Much calcium Do We Need?

NHS Foundation Trust recommends		
Infants	0-12 months	525mg
Children	1-3 years	350mg
	4-6 years	450mg
	7-10 years	550mg
Boys	11-18 years	1,000mg
Girls	11-18 years	800mg
Adults	19+ years	700mg
Pregnancy		700mg
Breastfeeding		1,200mg
Adults	Osteoporosis/osteopenia	1,200mg
Adults	Coeliac Disease up to 55 years	1,000mg
Adults	Coeliac Disease 55+ years	1,200mg

Doctors often recommend that a postmenopausal woman consumes 1,500mg of calcium a day.

Calcium Fortified Foods v Calcium-rich Foods

There is a big difference!

Calcium Fortified Foods

Calcium fortified foods are those that have a calcium supplement added to them - it doesn't naturally occur in the food.

Fortified food carries all the risks of taking calcium supplements.

Manufacturers are aware that consumers often seek foods high in calcium and some fortify their products with calcium supplements, which some people might confuse with naturally occurring calcium.

Some types of cereal are fortified and can deliver up to 1,000mg (100% of the recommended daily intake, for some people) per serving.

Common foods fortified with calcium are: bread, cereals, soya milk, rice milk and orange juice, some tortillas and crackers.

Soya milk is often praised for its high calcium content, but it is actually mostly high in calcium due to the calcium carbonate that is dissolved into it! This may be more convenient than taking separate supplements but at the end of the day the calcium is not naturally occurring, so consumers are no better off and left with the chalk or cheese decision again.

Also, if you are taking calcium supplements in addition to eating food that is fortified with calcium you need to be careful that you are not ending up taking too much supplement. Remember it's possible to overdose on calcium supplement (pills or calcium-fortified food), but you are unlikely to overdose on naturally occurring calcium in food.

Calcium-rich foods

You may opt to obtain your calcium in food naturally (meaning without resorting to calcium fortified foods and instead eat foods naturally rich in calcium).

Foods that are particularly high in calcium include cow's milk, goat's milk, yoghurt, cheese, some grains and some vegetables.

Dairy products made from low-fat cow's milk will also be rich in calcium.

If you cannot consume dairy foods you will need to include certain grains and vegetables in your diet. Look for naturally occurring calcium!

Covering both your options

You may wish to take your calcium supplements as well as eating a diet rich in calcium.

Invest in some kitchen scales

I suggest you buy yourself some kitchen scales.

The quantities I've listed below are convenient, and ideal for buying and putting together for meals.

Examples of Ways to Include 1,200mg of Calcium Daily

Below are examples of food combinations that contain 1,200mg calcium (this is often the recommended amount, and remember you can eat over the recommended amount of calcium if it's naturally occurring!)

Please note all calcium values in this book are approximate.

Suggestions for foods with high dairy content

All-Bran 40g		44mg calcium
Milk 400ml	(used on cereal & in tea/coffee)	564mg
Cheese 75g	(Cheddar, Monterey Jack, Gruyere, Mozzarella, Provolone, Edam, Gouda, Swiss)	560mg
Slice white bread x 2		130mg

Suggestions for foods with low fat content that also help with digestion.

(If you get constipated this combination will be beneficial.)

(Breakfast: All-Bran, flaxseed & Actimel)	
All-Bran 40g	44mg calcium
Flax seed (milled) 50g	85mg
Actimel 100g pot x 3	360mg
Avocado	30mg
Tin of Salmon (with bones) 105g	220mg
Egg (boiled or other)	25mg
Slice white bread x 2	130mg
Yogurt probiotic 140g pot x 2	280mg
Milk for tea/coffee x 4	50mg

Suggestions for vegan foods

All-Bran 40g	44mg calcium
Sesame seeds 50g	488mg
Chia seeds 158g	300mg
Avocado	30mg
Slice white bread x 2	130mg
Orange large	60mg
Kiwi	60mg
Fig x 3	100mg

Suggestions for low fat dairy

(Breakfast: All-Bran, chia seeds & milk)		
All-Bran 40g		44mg calcium
Chia seeds 158g		300mg
Milk (skimmed) 400ml	(used on cereal & in tea/coffee)	564mg
Quark 250g pot		300mg

Foods high in calcium to choose from to create your own combination

		calcium
Milk 100mg		120mg
Yogurt 125g		190mg
Cheese		
Quark pot 250g		300mg
Cottage Cheese pot 300g		250mg
Cheddar 75g		540mg
Monterey Jack 75g		558mg
Gruyere 75g		757mg
Mozzarella 75g		550mg
Provolone 75g		566mg
Edam 75g		550mg
Gouda 75g		525mg
Swiss 75g		592mg
Kidney Beans ½ tin		55mg
Edamame 100g		63mg
Avocado whole		30mg
Tomatoes ½ tin		68mg
Broccoli 100g		50mg
Green Beans 100g		40mg
Pak Choi 100g		105mg
Leeks 100g		60mg

	calcium
Chia seeds 25g	158mg
Flax seed (milled) 50g	127mg
Pumpkin seeds 50g	27mg
Sesame seeds 25g	244mg
Sunflower seed 50g	40mg
Almonds x 22 nuts	32mg
Hazelnuts x 22	32mg
Coconut Water (cup)	58mg
Figs x 3	100mg
Kiwi	60mg
Orange (large)	60mg
Apricot x 4	20mg
All-Bran 40mg	36mg
Bread (white slice)	65mg
Hummus ¼ pot	20mg
Baked beans (small tin)	120mg
Sweet Potato x 1 medium	40mg
Egg x 1	25mg
Prawns 150g	75mg

		calcium
Sardines tin (& bones) 120g		460mg
Salmon small tin (& bones) 105g		220mg

Recipes High in Calcium

Recipes by Gillian Greenwood, Audrey Goldberg and Daria Archilei

You can mix and match the ingredients as you wish because the calcium values are included. All calcium values are approximate and are rounded to the nearest mg.

Gillian's Recipes (The very quick ones)

All-Bran, flaxseed, chia & Actimel all help to keep you regular. Calcium supplements can make some people constipated. If you wish to combine supplements with calcium-rich foods you may be interested to find out which foods will help you combat constipation. All-Bran, flaxseed, chia seed and Actimel will all help. Below is a breakfast combination including all those foods. It is very high in calcium too.

All-Bran Breakfast

Total per person: 647mg calcium

Serves 1

- All-Bran 40g   (44mg calcium)
- Flaxseed (milled) 50g   (85mg calcium)
- Chia Seed (whole) 25g   (158mg calcium)
- Actimel Probiotic Yogurt drink 100g pot x 3   (360mg calcium)

Pour Flaxseed and Chia Seed into a bowl.
Shake the Actimel, open and pour on top.
Mix well.
Wait 5 mins then pour All-Bran into bowl.
Garnish with fruit if desired and eat immediately.
The timings keep the All-Bran crisp and the Flaxseed and Chia get time to soften a little.

Muesli Breakfast

Total per person: 830mg calcium

Serves 1

- Alpen sugar-free 68g (100mg calcium)
- Flaxseed (milled) 35g (40mg calcium)
- Actimel Probiotic Yogurt drink 100g pot x 3 (360mg calcium)
- Skimmed milk 250ml (330mg calcium)

You can use another sugar free muesli
Pour Muesli & Flaxseed into a bowl.
Shake the Actimel, open and pour on top.
Add 250ml skimmed milk.
Mix well, put in fridge **overnight** to soak up the milk & Actimel.
Garnish with fruit if desired before serving.
The timings allow the muesli to fully soak up the Actimel and skimmed milk. If you do not soak overnight, you will not need the skimmed milk.

Salmon Avocado Salad

Total per serving: 342mg calcium
Serves 1

- Salmon (tinned with bones) 105g   (220mg calcium)
- Egg boiled and sliced   (25mg calcium)
- Avocado
  (spooned out with teaspoon)   (30mg calcium)
- 2 Sliced Tomatoes   (25mg calcium)
- Green beans 100g   (40mg calcium)
- or Runner beans
- 1/4 bell pepper cubed   (2mg calcium)
- Lettuce
- Cucumber sliced
- Balsamic vinegar
- Olive Oil
- Salt & Pepper

Boil green beans.
Boil egg until hard boiled.
Place lettuce in dish (pre-washed prepared lettuce is so much quicker!).
Add tomatoes, cucumber, bell pepper & avocado.
Put contents of tin of salmon (including bones!) onto salad.
Drizzle vinegar & oil over salad & salmon.
Place egg onto salad and slice.
Place green beans on salad.
Add salt & pepper.

Cottage Cheese Green Beans Salad

Total per serving: 317mg calcium

Serves 1
- Cottage Cheese 300g   (250mg calcium)
- 2 Sliced Tomatoes   (25mg calcium)
- Green beans 100g   (40mg calcium)
- or Runner beans
- 1/4 bell pepper cubed   (2mg calcium)
- Lettuce
- Cucumber sliced
- Balsamic vinegar
- Olive Oil
- Salt & Pepper

Boil green beans.
Place lettuce in dish (pre-washed prepared lettuce is so much quicker!).
Add tomatoes, cucumber, bell pepper.
Drizzle vinegar & oil over salad & salmon.
Place green beans on salad.
Add salt & pepper.

Spicy Salmon Avocado

Total per person: 606mg calcium

Serves 1

- Tin of salmon with bones 213g   (440mg calcium)
- Tin chopped tomatoes   (136mg calcium)
- 1 avocado   (30mg calcium)
- Diced cucumber
- Pinch salt, pepper
- Cayenne pepper to taste

Microwave contents of a tin of tomatoes 2 mins full power with the salt & pepper. Put in a dish.
Add tinned salmon, avocado & cucumber.
Add sprinkle of cayenne pepper and serve.

Strawberry Mousse

Total per person: 100mg calcium

Serves 3

- 250g quark - 1 tub   (300mg calcium)
- 125g strawberries frozen (or any summer fruits: raspberries/cranberries/blackberries...)
- 25g icing sugar (if you have a sweet tooth)
- lemon juice – tablespoon (to taste)

Mix Quark, Sugar and Lemon Juice in a bowl.
Add frozen fruit and stir.
Spoon into desert bowls and serve.

Daria Archilei's Recipes

Learn from an Italian how to cook recipes from around the world

Sardine Pasta

Total per person: 731mg calcium

Serves 2

- Sardines 300g (canned in oil)   (1146 mg calcium)
- Pine nuts 20g   (8mg calcium)
- Tomato x 1 tin   (136mg calcium)
- Shallot x 1   (7.5mg calcium)
- Garlic x 1 clove   (16mg calcium)
- Parsley 100g   (138mg calcium)
- Pasta 160g   (10mg calcium)
- Extra Virgin Olive oil 1 tablespoon
- Salt & Pepper
- Chilli 1 fresh
- Black Pepper 1 pinch

Remove the oil from the Sardines. Warm the Olive Oil in a frying pan & add Sardines, Shallots, Garlic & chilli. Add tomato, pinch Salt, pinch of Pepper & Pine Nuts and simmer on low heat. In a saucepan boil 1½ litres of water with a pinch of salt for approx. 9 mins (al dente). Drain water from Pasta. Add finely chopped Parsley to the Sardine mixture. Add Pasta to Sardine mixture and stir. Return to the heat and simmer for 2 mins more.

Vegan Curry

Total per person: 371mg calcium

Serves 2

- Soya chunks 200g (soaked in water) (554 mg calcium)
- Turmeric 2 teaspoons (2mg calcium)
- Cumin 2 teaspoons (10mg calcium)
- Garam masala 1 teaspoon
- Potatoes 100g (65mg calcium)
- Tomato x 2 (25mg calcium)
- Courgette x 1 (31mg calcium)
- Salt 1 pinch
- Chilli x 2
- Garlic clove x 1 (16mg calcium)
- Onion x 1 (25mg calcium)
- Coconut oil 2 teaspoons
- Chopped Coriander 20g (13.5mg calcium)

Soak the Soya Chunks in water for at least 30 mins.
Slice the Onion, Courgette & Potatoes.
Chop the tomatoes.
Lightly fry the Onion, Garlic, Chilli & Cumin in the Coconut Oil.
After 4 mins add the Tomatoes, Turmeric & Garam Masala.
After 4 more mins add the sliced Potatoes & Courgette.
Add I cup Water & pinch of Salt and continue cooking for 15 mins until light brown.
Remove Soya Chunks from their water & add to the pan.

Once all the ingredients are in the pan cook for 30 min on low heat.
Add extra Chilli (to taste) & chopped Coriander.

Fennel Salad

Total per person: 64mg calcium

Serves 2

- Fennel 200g (98mg calcium)
- Orange 50g (20mg calcium)
- Black olives 20g (10.5mg calcium)
- Olive oil 1 tablespoon
- Salt 1 pinch
- Black pepper 1 pinch

Remove the pits from the Olives.
Slice the Fennel very finely. Peel the oranges & cut between the membranes to segment the orange, retaining any juices.
Mix the Orange with Fennel, Olive Oil, Black Olives & Salt & Pepper.
Ideal for a side dish.

Caprese with Pesto

Total per person: 424.5mg calcium

Serves 2

- Buffalo Mozzarella 100g (731mg calcium)
- Tomatoes 100g (10mg calcium)
- Pesto: Fresh Basil 50g (88.5mg calcium)
- Pine Nuts 1 tablespoon (8g) (3mg calcium)
- Garlic 1 clove (16mg calcium)
- Parmesan Cheese 50g (0.5mg calcium)
- Olive Oil 1 tablespoon
- Pinch Salt & Pepper

Slice the Tomatoes and Buffalo Mozzarella & arrange on a serving plate.

To save time you could put your Pesto ingredients into a blender, otherwise mix thoroughly until you reach a smooth consistency. Spoon the Pesto onto the Mozzarella in an attractive pattern.

This makes a quick, healthy lunch on its own or as an accompaniment to a main course.

Prawns with Parsley Sauce Starter

Total per person: 267mg calcium

Serves 2

- 200g Prawns (380mg calcium)
- 100g Parsley (138mg calcium)
- Lettuce leaf for garnish
- 1 Garlic Clove (16mg calcium)
- 1 Fresh Chilli
- Extra Virgin Olive Oil 1 tablespoon
- Pinch Salt & Pepper

Boil Prawns for 3 mins, rinse and allow to cool.

Sauce:
Using a blender mix Parsley, Garlic, Chilli, Oil, Salt & Pepper. Place lettuce on plate, arrange prawns on top. Pour green sauce over some of the prawns/lettuce.

Bruschetta with Goats Cheese & Tomatoes

Total per person: 314mg calcium

Serves 2

- 200g Bread Toasted　　　(206mg calcium)
- 2 Sliced Tomatoes　　　(24.5mg calcium)
- 100g Goats Cheese　　　(298mg calcium)
- 50g Basil coarsely chopped　(88.5mg calcium)
- Black olives 20g　　　　(10.5mg calcium)
- Extra Virgin Olive Oil 1 teaspoonful

Toast bread.
Thickly spread goats' cheese onto toast.
Add the sliced tomatoes black olives.
Drizzle the olive oil and sprinkle basil on top.

Berry & Chia Seed Porridge

Total per person: 322.5mg calcium

Serves 1

- Chia seeds 1 tablespoon   (67mg calcium)
- Milk half glass (full fat)   (236mg calcium)
- Yogurt 1 tablespoon   (11mg calcium)
- Berries 100g   (6mg calcium)
- Almond butter 1 teaspoon   (2.5mg calcium)
- or Almond 10g

Mix the Chia Seeds, Yogurt and milk in a bowl and stir.
Chill for several hours in the fridge, ideally overnight.
Decorate with berries & almond butter.

Ricotta Mousse with Almond Butter

Total per person: 160.5mg calcium

Serves 2

- 150g Ricotta Cheese   (310mg calcium)
- Raw Cacao 15g (1 tablespoon)
- Almond Butter (1 tablespoon)   (5.5mg calcium)
- Almond Flakes for decoration (1 teaspoon)   (5.5mg calcium)

In a blender mix Ricotta Cheese, Cacao & Almond Butter.
When consistency is smooth pour into individual dishes and decorate with Almond Flakes.
Chill for 1 hour in Fridge.

Audrey Goldberg's Recipes

Learn from Le Cordon Bleu Chef Audrey how to create exciting new dishes

Pretty in Pink Prawns with Marie Rose Sauce

Total per person: 190mg calcium per serving

Serves 2

- 280g cooked and shelled prawns   (100mg calcium)
- Salt and black pepper to taste
- Seasoning of choice e.g. Moroccan spices
- Marie Rose sauce, see recipe below   (50mg calcium)
- 2 baby gem lettuces   (60 mg calcium)
- 1 small radicchio (use whole leaves)   (60mg calcium)
- 1 red endive (use whole leaves)   (60mg calcium)
- Pretty in Pink Dressing (see recipe)   (50mg calcium)
- Coriander
- Mint
- Lemon zest
- Edible dried rose petals (optional)

Marie Rose Sauce

(50mg calcium)

- 1/2 cup mayonnaise   (10mg calcium)
- 1/2 cup ketchup   (10mg calcium)
- Salt and pepper to taste
- 2 tsp Worcestershire sauce   (30mg calcium)
- Dash of brandy (optional)
- 2 squeezes of lemon juice
- Touch of Tabasco
- Pinch of sugar
- Lasts up to 2 days in the fridge

Pretty in Pink Dressing
(50mg calcium)

- 1/3 cup raspberry vinegar or white wine vinegar, spun with a large handful of fresh raspberries   (30mg calcium)
- 1 cup light olive oil
- 1 tsp seeded mustard
- 1 tbs Demerara or brown sugar   (10mg calcium)
- 2 tbs fresh lemon juice
- 2 tbs light soy sauce   (10mg calcium)
- Salt and coarse black pepper to taste

Whisk dressing ingredients together except oil.
Slowly add oil, whisking continuously.

Wash leaves, separate and keep them intact.
Season and toss leaves, displaying the pinky red ones in the pink dressing.
Arrange decoratively in a bowl.
Coat seasoned prawns lavishly with Marie Rose sauce and pile into leaves.
Add coriander, mint and lemon zest.
Add rose petals.

Scrambled Egg with Gravlax and Mascarpone

Total per person: 164mg calcium

Serves 2

- 4 eggs   (100mg calcium)
- Salt and coarsely ground black pepper to taste
- Handful (7g) of fresh basil leaves for eggs   (12.5mg calcium)
- Fresh basil leaves to garnish 3g   (5mg calcium)
- 200g (1 small packet) gravlax or smoked salmon (salmon 22mg calcium)
- Squeeze of lemon juice
- Black pepper to taste
- Small handful (2g) of dill
  (4mg calcium)
- 1 avocado, thinly sliced
  (24mg calcium)
- Squeeze of lime juice
- 1/2 cup mascarpone
  cheese 60g (80mg calcium)
- 2 tsp lemon juice to taste
- Sprinkle of lemon zest
- 2 slices of brown bread,
  toasted (80mg calcium)

Beat eggs in a bowl until light and fluffy and season to taste.
Add whole basil leaves.
Scramble at a medium heat until just cooked through.
Serve on brown bread.
Place 2 large slices of gravlax or salmon decoratively next to each portion of scrambled egg. Season with lemon juice and black pepper.
Garnish with dill and basil leaves.
Add avocado and lime juice if required.
Mix the mascarpone with the lemon juice.
Sprinkle with lemon zest.
Serve on the side, in a small bowl.

Tart Wild Mushroom

Total per person: 873.5mg calcium

Serves 4

- 400g wild mushrooms (Natoora or any wild mushrooms) (12mg calcium)
- Salt and coarsely ground black pepper
- 2 tsp seeded mustard (12mg calcium)
- Lightly oiled pan
- 4 tbs oil and soy mix (1/4 cup oil to 1 tbs Kikkoman Less Salt Soy Sauce) (10mg calcium)
- Cooking oil if required
- 1 (320g) packet puff pastry with butter (Pâte Feuilletée gives an excellent result. Jus-Rol puff pastry, preferably with butter, also good) (32mg calcium)
- 1/2 packet of grated Parmesan cheese 50g (freshly grated Parmesan is tastier) (555mg calcium)
- 2 tsp dried thyme (30mg calcium)
- Handful fresh or dried thyme 10g (4mg calcium)
- 10 thin Parmesan curls for decor, using a cheese slicer 20g (220mg calcium)

Follow the pastry instructions on the box.
Prick all over with a fork.
Place in a medium-sized non-stick frying pan or a non-stick baking sheet.
Place in a preheated 200°C oven and bake blind for approximately 15 minutes or until golden. Reduce heat if necessary. Do not worry if it rises slightly.
Remove from oven.

Cook the seasoned mushrooms with oil and soy mix and mustard in an oiled pan for a few minutes on a medium heat until just cooked through. Add more oil or soy mix and cooking oil if required. You should be left with a little syrupy liquid in the pan.

Just before placing on the pastry, add cheese and dried thyme and mix gently. Place on the pastry in the pan.
Bake for 30-45 minutes until golden and crispy at 200°C. If necessary, reduce heat to 180°C and cook for longer.
Remove from baking sheet and place on a decorative plate. Sprinkle with freshly crushed or dried thyme leaves and parmesan curls (see below).

Place whole sprigs of thyme in a small pan and heat in a 180°C oven until crispy and fragrant. Crush over the tart, along with the parmesan curls.

Cut with a sharp serrated knife or with a scissors or a pizza slicer

Salmon Theoule sur Mer with Gremolata

Total per person: 45mg calcium

Serves 4

- 4 medium-sized salmon steaks, minimum 150g each, bottom skin intact (54mg calcium)
- Salt of choice
- 1 tbs Moroccan spice (or any spices of your choice)
- 1/3 cup Panko crumbs 25g
- 1/3 cup almond flour 25g (66mg calcium)
- Squeeze of oil and soy mix (1/2 cup oil to 2 tbs Kikkoman Less Salt Sauce or any low salt soy sauce) (10.5mg calcium)
- Chopped parsley
- Lemon rind
- Gremolata (see below)

Salmon

Lightly rinse salmon.
Place the pieces in a dish and pat dry with kitchen towel.
Season with salt on each side of flesh and skin.
Mix the crumbs and flour together.
Add the Moroccan spice and gently pack onto the flesh and skin of the fish, pressing gently with your fingers.
Place in the fridge for a few hours to consolidate. The drier the crumbs, the crispier they will be after pan frying.
Remove from the fridge and bring to room temperature.
Heat non-stick pan to medium heat before frying the fish.

Cook flesh side down for 3-4 minutes or until crisp and golden. Check after 3 minutes. When a good colour, flip and cook skin side down for another 3-4 minutes. Look again after three minutes to check it is not overcooking. It should be just cooked through. A small steak will take approximately 6-7 minutes, a medium steak approximately 7-8 minutes or a large steak approx. 9-10 minutes, depending on the hob heat, the pan size and the size and shape of the salmon pieces. (It's also handy to fry one extra steak, cut it open and check that it's slightly undercooked, or just cooked through). If they look dry at any point, squeeze with a little oil.

Serve with the following gremolata if you wish, otherwise use chopped parsley and lemon rind.

Gremolata

- Handful of samphire, cut thinly (seasonal) 5g   (8mg calcium)
- Handful of dill, chopped finely 3g   (6mg calcium)
- Handful of sultanas, thinly sliced 5g
- Handful of parsley, finely chopped 5g   (30mg calcium)
- 2 mint sprigs, finely chopped   (5mg calcium)

Mix, lightly, all together with your fingers and sprinkle lavishly on the salmon flesh. Serve immediately.

Affogato

Total per person: 451mg calcium

Serves 1

- 80g (2 large scoops) of creamy vanilla ice cream (keep frozen). (You can scoop the balls in advance and store them in the deep freeze) (95mg calcium)
- 1 shot espresso (1/2 shot if you find it too strong)
- 100g chocolate, finely chopped (101mg calcium)
- 200mls double cream (140mg calcium)
- 60g toasted peanuts (Nuts Pick Online are a good choice) (55mg calcium)
- Check that they are not too salty. If so, use less, if unsalted, add a little sea salt. You can also use any other nuts of your choice.
- 2 teaspoons of sesame seeds on top (60mg calcium)
- 1-2 tbls of Amaretto, Disaronno, Frangelico, or Kahlua liqueur (to taste)

Chocolate Sauce

Melt the cream at a very low heat in a double boiler or heavy-bottomed pot to prevent curdling.
Stir constantly.
Remove from heat when it starts reaching the boil. (Bubbles will appear on the outer rims of the pot.)
Add finely chopped chocolate.
Stir until combined and unctuous.
If too thick, add a teaspoon or two of boiling water.
Serve as soon as possible.

To serve

Place ice cream in decorative bowl.
Either pour hot coffee, over the ice cream or pour into the bottom of the bowl with the ice cream on top.
Put some warm chocolate sauce over it.
Sprinkle on the toasted nuts and sesame seeds.
Add a dollop of liqueur if you wish.

The chocolate sauce can be reheated in the microwave, with 2 tsp water, to warm, for a few seconds.
Stir 2 - 3 times to prevent scalding or curdling.
Serve immediately.

Eastern Mess

Total per person: 197mg calcium

Serves 2

- 4 large meringues from a bakery or a supermarket.
- 80g vanilla ice cream (4 scoops) (95mg calcium)
- 3 large punnets of raspberries (2 for the sauce) approximately 375g (94mg calcium)
- 1/4 cup caster sugar
- Lemon juice (if required)
- 2 tbs Creme de Cassis liqueur or any other fruit liqueur or fruit juice e.g. orange juice (optional)
- 1 tbsp pomegranate seeds
- 12g (2 tbsp) sesame seeds (80mg calcium)
- 12g pistachios (120mg calcium)
- 5 leaves basil (5mg calcium)
- Ras el hanout (North African spice)
- Edible dried rose petals (optional)
- Raspberry Sauce

Spin 2 punnets of raspberries and sugar in a or blender.
Add liqueur if you wish. Taste for sweetness. Add lemon juice (to taste). Set aside.

To serve

Place 2 lightly crushed meringues in each decorative bowl.
Place 2 scoops of ice cream on each meringue.
Pour generously over raspberry sauce.
Add extra raspberries.
Add pomegranate seeds, sesame seeds and pistachios.
Lightly sprinkle with Ras el hanout.
Add basil and rose petals for garnishing.

Deconstructed Cheesecake with Figs

Total per person: 361.5mg calcium

Serves 2

- 200g original Philadelphia cream cheese (196mg calcium)
- 3 tbs kefir drink (fermented milk) (66mg calcium)
- 1 tbs caster sugar
- Sprinkle of lemon zest
- 1 tsp vanilla essence or extract
- 2 (36g) crushed digestive biscuits (28mg calcium)
- Sesame seeds 5g (40g calcium)
- 4 fresh figs, halved (108mg)
- 4 whole figs (108mg)
- 6 dried figs (162mg)
- 750ml bottle red wine
- 3/4 cup caster sugar
- Fresh thyme 5g (2mg calcium)
- 1 vanilla pod or 1 tsp vanilla essence (0.5mg calcium)
- Fresh mint leaves 5g (12.5mg calcium)

Mix the first five ingredients together in a bowl.
Place in a decorative bowl.
Pour the mixed biscuits and seeds on top of the cheese. Set aside a few to garnish.
Can be refrigerated.
Take out of fridge an hour before serving.

Pour wine, sugar, thyme and vanilla into a small pot.
Simmer until the sauce reduces and thickens.
Lightly poach the halved fresh figs until coloured and sticky for about 8 minutes.
Remove the figs from the sauce and set aside.

Continue reducing the sauce until sticky.
Set aside and keep warm.

To serve

Arrange the poached figs on room temperature cheesecake.
Pour over sticky wine sauce generously.
Add whole and dried figs which have been halved.
Add a sprinkle of sesame seeds.
Dress with a few mint leaves.

Salmon Rissoles

Total per person: 265mg calcium

Serves 2

- 213g John West wild pacific red salmon with bones & juices (469mg calcium)
- 1/2 tsp coarse black pepper
- 2 tsp Moroccan spice (or spice of choice)
- 2 pinches of chilli flakes
- 2 tbs oil
- 2 tsp lemon juice
- 2 tbs panko breadcrumbs
- 1 egg (25mg calcium)
- 2 tsp (2g) chopped coriander (2.5g calcium)
- 2 tsp (2g) chopped parsley (12mg calcium)
- 2 tsp (2g) chopped mint (5mg calcium)
- 2 tbs extra bread crumbs for coating
- a pinch of lemon rind for garnishing
- 2 tbs extra mixed, chopped herbs for garnishing
- 2g coriander, 2g parsley, 1g mint (17mg calcium)

Section the salmon into fairly large chunks.
Place in bowl together with skin, bones & juice.
Combine the remaining ingredients, except the extra crumbs, extra herbs and lemon rind.
Roll into medium sized rissoles, pat gently and dip into the extra crumbs.
Place in fridge for an hour or two.
Bring to room temperature before pan frying.
Lightly coat bottom of fairly small stick free pan with cooking oil.
Pan fry at medium heat for 2-3 minutes on each side or until golden brown.

Serve immediately, sprinkled with lemon rind and extra herbs.

Serve with Tomato and Bean Salsa (see following recipe).

Tomato and Beans Salsa

Total per person: 118mg calcium

Serves 4

- 300g plum tomatoes, sliced in half (300mg calcium)
- 30g edamame beans (bought frozen from the supermarket) (20mg calcium)
- 1/4 tsp salt
- 1/4 tsp coarse pepper
- 1/8th tsp chilli flakes
- 1/2 thinly sliced red onion (30mg calcium)
- 1 tsp sesame seeds (88mg calcium)
- 1 tsp cumin seeds (20mg calcium)
- 5g flat leaf parsley (approximately 2 tbs) (10mg calcium)

- 5 g fresh coriander (approximately 2 tbs) (3mg calcium)
- 2 tbs extra virgin olive oil
- 2 tsp lemon or lime juice (add more dressing if required)
- 1/4-1/2 tsp lemon zest

- Optional
- 2 tbs pomegranate seeds
- 2 tsp toasted pine nuts (1.5mg calcium)

Mix all ingredients together gently, leaving out a few herbs for garnishing.

Spaghetti Bolognese with Pesto

Total per person: 188.5mg calcium (without pesto)
276.5mg calcium (with pesto)

Serves 4

Pasta

- 250g spaghetti or linguine (17.5 mg calcium)
- water
- 2-4 tsp coarse salt
- 2 tbs oil
- Few shakes of oil
- 1 tbs salt, to taste
- 2 tsp coarse black pepper, to taste

Bring water in a deep medium pot to a rolling boil on the hob.
Add lightly rinsed pasta to the water.
Cover and simmer for approximately 10 minutes, until the pasta is "al dente", or firm to the bite.
Pour into a sieve.
Rinse lightly in tepid water.
Place back in warm pan.
Add a few shakes of oil.
Season with salt and pepper.

Serve immediately with the Bolognese. (with optional pesto alongside).

Bolognese

- 1/4 cup oil
- 2 large red onions, thinly sliced   (300mg calcium)
- 1 large carrot, thinly sliced   (23mg calcium)
- Salt to taste
- Pepper to taste
- 1/2 cup oil and soya mix (1/2 cup oil with 2 tbs low salt soy sauce) divided into two
- 500g low fat beef mince   (10.5mg calcium)
- 2 tsp beef stock powder or salt of choice to taste
- 1/4 tsp coarse ground black pepper to taste
- Oil and soy mix (the remaining amount)

- Cooking oil if required

Add 1/4 cup oil to the bottom of a deep pot.
Season onions and carrot with salt and pepper to taste.
Toss in half the oil and soy mix.
Lightly brown the onions and carrots in a medium sized pot on the hob.
Mix the seasoned mince together and spritz with the remaining oil and soy mix and add to pan with browned vegetables.
Add more oil if required.
Cook, uncovered, until lightly browned.

Add tomato sauce ingredients
- 1 chopped tin of tomatoes (136mg calcium)
- 3 tsp chicken stock powder
- 1 tsp light soy sauce (5mg calcium)
- 1 tbs brown sugar or sweetener of choice
- 1 tsp Pommery mustard or any seeded mustard (6mg calcium)
- 1 tsp fresh chilli
- 1/4 cup soaked and chopped dried porcini (optional)
- 1 tin of borlotti or cannellini beans without liquid (210mg calcium)
- 2 tbs red wine or bean liquid
- Simmer gently, covered for approximately 1 hour or until tender.

Place a portion of pasta on a decorative plate, topping generously with the Bolognese.
Add a few basil leaves and pine nuts.
Serve pesto separately. Recipe on following page.

If you do not have pesto, add a few shavings of parmigiano reggiano, pine nuts or basil, otherwise purchase pesto from a supermarket.

It deep freezes perfectly.
Can also add pancetta or chopped, cooked chicken livers if required.

Pesto

Total per person: 88mg calcium

Serves 4
- 2 cups packed basil leaves 40g   (71mg calcium)
- 1 tsp roast or fresh garlic 15mg   (32mg calcium)
- 1/4 cup toasted pine nuts 75g   (30mg calcium)
- Handful toasted walnuts 10g   (10mg calcium)
- Handful fresh rocket. 6g   (10mg calcium)
- 1/2 tsp chicken stock powder, Maldon salt or any salt of your choice
- 1/4 tsp freshly ground black pepper
- 1/2 cup (45g) freshly grated parmigiano reggiano (parmesan) (499mg calcium)
- 2/3 cup virgin olive oil

Add all ingredients together, in a blender or Magimix and pulse until smooth.

Wonderful with Spaghetti Bolognese, pasta, soup, artichokes, asparagus and a variety of salads.

Sardine Sarnie

Total per person: 369mg calcium

Serves 2
- 2 tins sardines with bones and olive oil (650mg calcium)
- 1/3 Cup Hellmann's real Mayonnaise
- 1 /2 tsp Dijon mustard (3mg calcium)
- Sprinkle of coarse black pepper
- 2 thinly sliced olives (5mg calcium)
- 4 thinly sliced capers
- 2 slices of toasted brown bread (80mg calcium)
- 2 small pickled cucumbers
- English mustard

Serve the sardines whole with bones and oil.
Mix remaining 5 ingredients and serve separately in a little pot.
Can also be mashed, if preferred.
Serve with toasted brown bread, cucumber and mustard.

Breakfast Bomb

Total per person: 1026mg calcium
Serves 1

- 1 bottle 0 percent Actimel (120mg calcium)
- 160 gm Kefir yoghurt (177mg calcium)
- Splash of Kefir original (fermented milk drink)
- 2 heaped tbs (30g) of any combination of the following nuts, herbs and seeds from prepared Linwoods packs.
- These include flaxseed, sunflower, pumpkin, sesame seeds, goji berries or almond and brazil nut mix, or hempseed, oat bran with chia seeds and/or goji berries

Smoothie

- 1 banana   (6 mg calcium)
- 1 small mango   (37 mg calcium)
- Juice of 1 orange   (10 mg calcium)
- 4 passion fruits. Reserve 2 for garnishing   (5 mg calcium)
- Basil leaves (3g) for garnishing   (5 mg calcium)

Combine all the fruits, setting 2 passion fruits and basil leaves aside. Spin in Magimix or Nutribullet.

Drink Actimel, good for the gut.
Mix together the yoghurt and Kefir products.
Add 2 heaped tbs of the mixed Linseed packs and/or oat bran and/or chia seeds and/or goji berries.
Drink or pour the smoothie over the breakfast bomb, adding the reserved passion fruits and a few basil leaves for garnish.

Shakshuka

Total per person: 817mg calcium

Serves 2
- 4 sliced onions (80mg calcium)
- 1 thinly sliced red pepper (7mg calcium)
- Season with chicken stock powder, Maldon salt or natural sea salt
- 4 tbsp oil and soy mix (1 tbsp light soy to 4 tbsp olive oil)
- Cooking oil
- 2 tins chopped tomatoes (reserve juice) (136mg calcium)
- 1 1/2 tsp chicken stock powder or salt
- 1/2 tsp ground black pepper
- 2 tsp light soy sauce
- 2 tbs demerara or brown sugar
- 1 tsp chopped red chillies
- 1 clove garlic, finely chopped
- 5 large eggs (125mg calcium)
- 1/2 cup grated feta cheese (370g calcium)
- 1/4 cup tahini, thinned with a little water (256g calcium)
- 500g natural yoghurt (650mg calcium)
- Salt and pepper to taste
- 5g fresh coriander (3mg calcium)
- 5g fresh parsley (7mg calcium)
- Ras el hanout (a North African spice). It is available from the supermarket
- Edible dried rose petals (available from food specialist shops, optional)

Cook seasoned onions and red peppers with oil and soy mix, in a medium nonstick frying pan, until softened and lightly browned.
Add cooking oil if required.
Add tomatoes, salt and pepper, soy sauce, sugar, chillies and garlic.
Cook for a few minutes until reduced and fairly thick to accommodate the eggs.
When still hot, make little dips in the sauce and gently break an egg into each dip. Add 1/4 cup of the grated feta cheese. Set aside the remainder for garnishing.

Simmer gently for approximately 15 minutes, covered, until the whites are set and the yolks are runny. Instead of using the hob, you can place the saucepan into a 180°C oven in the centre of the oven, for approximately 10 - 20 minutes, with the lid on, to set the eggs. Keep checking that the eggs do not overcook. If necessary, remove the lid. They are ready when the whites are cooked through. The yolks should be slightly runny when serving.

When ready, add the remaining grated feta cheese.
Drizzle tahini and yoghurt, mixed together in a small dish, lightly over the dish.
Add fresh coriander and parsley.
Add a sprinkle of Ras el Hanout.
Add rose petals to garnish.

About the Authors

Gillian Greenwood

Gillian is a Pilates Yoga Teacher, Absolute Beginners Ballet Teacher, Masseuse, Stress Management and Lifestyle Consultant. She has been teaching in Chelsea and surrounding areas in London UK for some 30 years and more recently on Zoom. This is her second book. In 2006 she wrote 'Pilates & Lifestyle with a Foreword by Julian Clary'.

Gillian has always tried to eat healthily but first became interested in calcium after fracturing her foot in 2014. She was advised to take calcium supplements but decided to do some research on the internet. After a considerable time searching, she devised a way to eat the required daily 1,200mg calcium instead of taking calcium supplements. She searched on the internet for books, calcium recipes and diets but couldn't find any. She then looked up which foods were high in calcium. It was a mammoth task. It is not easy to find foods that one can put into a daily diet. The values are sometimes quoted in 60mg, 100mg, a handful, sometimes as a cup full etc...! All were different values; impossible to compare without first calculating how much calcium in the same number of grams for all the foods. Something she thought might take a few minutes ended up taking days! To save you time and inconvenience Gillian decided to write this book with her friend and client Cordon Bleu Chef Audrey Goldberg and her friend and nutrition advisor Daria Archilei.

Audrey Goldberg

Gillian, my extraordinary ballet and tap-dancing teacher, who is a specialist and guru in her field, has asked me to collaborate with her in writing some simple recipes which are fun to eat, easy to execute and are rich in calcium content.

I was born in Port Elizabeth, South Africa on a beautiful bay, with a blue flag sea and salty winds which blew in a wealth of smells and culinary dreams. The waters were rich in grunter, leer fish and the like, not to mention the crab and giant oysters. These molluscs were roughly shucked by my father, Gaby, rinsed under a tap in the garden and were then, with heads flung back, gulped down gluttonously by the family. The tentacles of culinary magic had taken their grip.

Education at Collegiate School for Girls, a renowned school in the Eastern Cape, led to graduating 3 years later in Social Science at the University of Cape Town and then a move to Johannesburg, to shape my destiny.

I met and married my husband, Peter, four years later. I decided after 10 years and having had a son and a daughter, that I needed to spread my culinary wings. Le Cordon Bleu South Africa followed (with international recognition) and developed a few years later into a homemade cookery school, TV appearances, magazine interviews and articles.

The birth of another son and political unrest in South Africa, influenced the family's decision to move to London. We have lived here, happily, with our now adult children and grandchildren for almost twenty years.

The recipes brim with passion and sometimes cheek. You will find a complexity of flavours with a strong sense of colour, form, texture and of course, calcium.

Food is a powerful life force which propels us on our journey. It feeds our mind with healthy information. This has a spiritual and energising effect on body, spirit and soul. So, read, eat, make and enjoy it to the core.

Daria Archilei

Daria is a nutrition and health consultant.

Born in 1990 in Spoleto Umbria, Italy, she has lived in the UK since 2015.

She worked as an Advanced Health Advisor in Holland and Barrett in Fulham Road for five years. Since 2016 she completed Product Advisor Qualification from Holland and Barrett (2017) (Herbal remedies, aromatherapy, vitamins and minerals, basic ailments) and Advanced Product Advisor Qualification from Holland and Barrett (2018) (Body system, amino-acids, weight management, nutrition, sports nutrition, food and drink). Also, in 2020 she completed Internationally Accredited by CDP Diploma in Nutrition, Health and Wellness and Dietary Supplement Advisor.

Her passion for nutrition leads her to help her friends and customers to improve their daily diet and enjoy healthy food.

Thanks to her friend Gillian, she uses her knowledge about vitamins and minerals to develop calcium recipes you can enjoy with your family and friends.

Editing and Technical Support

Editing and Technical support including editing, typesetting, submission to Amazon was provided by Lee McLoughlin

Recipes Index

Affogato, 48
All-Bran Breakfast, 24
Berry & Chia Seed Porridge, 37
Breakfast Bomb, 62
Bruschetta with Goats Cheese & Tomatoes, 36
Caprese with Pesto, 34
Deconstructed Cheesecake with Figs, 52
Eastern Mess, 50
Exercise, 14
Fennel Salad, 33
Muesli Breakfast, 25
Pesto, 60
Prawns with Parsley Sauce Starter, 35
Pretty in Pink Prawns with Marie Rose Sauce, 39
Ricotta Mousse with Almond Butter, 38
Salmon Avocado Salad, 26
Salmon Rissoles, 54
Salmon Theoule sur Mer with Gremolata, 46
Sardine Pasta, 31
Sardine Sarnie, 61
Scrambled Egg with Gravlax and Mascarpone, 42
Spaghetti Bolognese with Pesto, 58
Spicy Salmon Avocado, 28
Strawberry Mousse, 29
Tart Wild Mushroom, 44
Tomato and Beans Salsa, 56
Vegan Curry, 32

Printed in Great Britain
by Amazon